MODERN ROLE MODELS

Sheryl Swoopes

Karen Schweitzer

Mason Crest Publishers

Produced by OTTN Publishing in association with
21st Century Publishing and Communications, Inc.

MASON CREST PUBLISHERS INC.
370 Reed Road
Broomall, Pennsylvania 19008
(866) MCP-BOOK (toll free)
www.masoncrest.com

Printed in the United States of America.

First Printing

9 8 7 6 5 4 3 2 1

Library of Congress Cataloging-in-Publication Data

Schweitzer, Karen.
    Sheryl Swoopes / by Karen Schweitzer.
        p. cm. — (Modern role models)
    Includes bibliographical references.
    ISBN-13: 978-1-4222-0491-7 (hardcover) — ISBN-13: 978-1-4222-0778-9 (pbk.)
    ISBN-10: 1-4222-0491-X (hardcover)
    1. Swoopes, Sheryl—Juvenile literature. 2. Basketball players—United States—
Biography—Juvenile literature. 3. Women basketball players—United States—
Biography—Juvenile literature. I. Title.
    GV884.S88S34 2009
    796.323092—dc22
    [B]   2008020412

Publisher's note:
All quotations in this book come from original sources, and contain the spelling
and grammatical inconsistencies of the original text.

CROSS-CURRENTS

In the ebb and flow of the currents of life we are each influenced
by many people, places, and events that we directly experience
or have learned about. Throughout the chapters of this book you
will come across **CROSS-CURRENTS** reference boxes. These
boxes direct you to a **CROSS-CURRENTS** section in the back
of the book that contains fascinating and informative sidebars
and related pictures. Go on. ▶▶

CONTENTS

At the 2004 Summer Olympic Games, Sheryl Swoopes leaps above Australia's top-scorer Penny Taylor during the women's basketball gold medal game, held August 28, 2004, in Athens, Greece. The U.S. Women's Olympic Basketball Team won its third consecutive gold medal with a 74-63 victory over Australia. The win gave Sheryl her third Olympic gold medal.

Three-Time Olympic Gold Medalist

SHERYL SWOOPES HAS ESTABLISHED HERSELF AS one of the greatest basketball players of all time. She was the star of her college team and the first person to be signed by the WNBA. In addition to winning gold and bronze medals at the FIBA World Championships, she has won three Olympic gold medals.

Her wins have made Sheryl one of the most accomplished and highest-paid female basketball players in history. But money and endorsements aren't what motivate Sheryl. Since she was seven years old, she has been playing basketball for one reason: because she loves the game. Her passion has led her to a record-breaking career filled with Most Valuable Player awards and top recognition in the United States and abroad.

⋙ TEAM USA ⋘

After leading her college team, Texas Tech University, to back-to-back Southwest Conference titles and an NCAA Women's Basketball Championship in 1993, Sheryl won numerous awards and was named National Player of the Year by nine different organizations. She had a Nike shoe named after her and was easily one of the most recognizable names in basketball.

But after graduating, Sheryl was a legend without a league. At the time there was no such thing as a professional women's basketball league in the United States. If she wanted to play basketball for an American team, her only option was the USA Basketball Women's Senior National Team, or Team USA, which competed in international competitions such as the Olympic Games.

Swoopes tried out for Team USA for the first time in the spring of 1995. To prepare, she played **pickup games** with amateurs at the rec center near her home. The unique training program worked. Sheryl made the team. It was a lucky break for her and for the team. Sheryl was fast, she could shoot, and she was eager to play.

⋙ PREPARING FOR THE OLYMPICS ⋘

Team USA began traveling almost immediately after Sheryl was selected to train for the Olympic Games. Its members practiced together, played 60 **exhibition games**, and did everything they could to promote women's basketball.

The dedication and commitment paid off. The U.S. Women's Olympic Basketball Team won the gold medal at the 1996 Olympic Games. Team USA also made the world take a second look at women's basketball. After the Olympics, five new professional women's basketball leagues were formed—including one that still exists in the United States, the WNBA.

CROSS-CURRENTS

To learn more about the history of women's basketball as played at the Olympic Games, read "Women's Basketball in the Olympics." Go to page 48. ▶▶

In an interview 10 years after the team's Olympic victory, head coach Tara VanDerveer commented on the 1996 team's impact:

❝I like to think this team was a catalyst that helped expose what's great about women's basketball, and how great the American women are. I think the process had begun somewhat to increase the popularity of the game, but this team helped to accelerate the process. **"**

➤ MORE SUCCESS AT THE OLYMPIC GAMES ◄

Sheryl initially declined the opportunity to play on the 2000 Olympic Team. She had a full schedule thanks to a new career in the WNBA and felt taking time off for the Olympic Games would mean taking more time off from her young son, Jordan. She posted a message on her Web site that read:

"There are not many things in life that mean more than a gold medal, but the upbringing of Jordan is

Sheryl Swoopes (far right) joins teammates as they celebrate winning their first gold medal at the 1996 Summer Olympics, held in Atlanta, Georgia. The other members of the U.S. Women's Olympic Basketball Team were Teresa Edwards, Dawn Staley, Ruthie Bolton, Jennifer Azzi, Lisa Leslie, Carla McGhee, Katy Steding, Katrina Felicia McClain, Rebecca Lobo, Venus Lacy, and Nikki McCray.

definitely one. A three-month commitment with significant international travel is just too much for Jordan and me. **"**

Sheryl had a change of heart later in the year, however, and was added to the team in June. As soon as the WNBA **playoffs** ended, she joined the squad to practice for the Olympics. The team went on to win a second gold medal.

Sheryl was again a member of the U.S. team at the 2000 Summer Olympics, held in Sydney, Australia. In this photograph, she defends against Slovakia's Zurana Zirkova during the quarterfinal game played on September 27. The United States would defeat Slovakia, 58-43, and go on to win its second gold medal at the final game against Australia.

➤ A SPECIAL WIN ◄

Sheryl was named to the U.S. Women's Olympic Basketball Team once again in 2004. Going into the Olympic Games, the team only had one goal: win the gold for the third straight time. The U.S. women were the favorite to win. There were three two-time Olympians playing for the team: Sheryl Swoopes, Dawn Staley, and Lisa Leslie.

CROSS-CURRENTS

If you'd like to know more about Lisa Leslie and Dawn Staley, check out "Sheryl's Olympic Teammates." Go to page 48. ▶▶

Not everyone thought Team USA was a sure thing. Some basketball observers suggested that the veterans might not be able to keep up with the younger players on other teams. Sheryl was 33 years old, Dawn Staley was 34, and Lisa Leslie was 32.

As it turned out, age was not a problem. Sheryl's performance throughout the Olympic Games was phenomenal. She led the 2004 Olympic team in three-point percentage (.429). She was also second in steals (19) and third in points per game (9.1), **assists** (13), and free throw percentage (.857). Lisa, Dawn, and the rest of Team USA performed just as well.

The U.S. team beat New Zealand, the Czech Republic, South Korea, Spain, China, Greece, and Russia to reach the final round. The last game was against Australia. In the end the U.S. women's team was able to clinch its third consecutive gold medal, beating Australia 74-63.

It was an amazing moment for Sheryl, Dawn, and Lisa. They became the only women in American history to win three consecutive Olympic basketball gold medals. Afterwards, Sheryl was quoted on the official Web site of the U.S. Olympic Committee explaining what the third medal meant to her:

> **❝This third one [gold medal] feels extremely good. I don't think there's many people out there who can say they won three gold medals at three Olympics in any sport. To be able to share this with all of my teammates, especially Dawn [Staley] and Lisa [Leslie] because we have been here before, make this one a little more special.❞**

A photomontage shows basketball player Sheryl Swoopes making a shot before a Texas background. Born and raised in the small town of Brownfield, in West Texas, she developed an interest in basketball from playing the game with older brothers James and Earl. At Brownfield High School Sheryl helped her team win the Texas Class 3A state championship in 1988.

Early Success on the Court

SHERYL DENISE SWOOPES WAS BORN ON MARCH 25, 1971, in the small town of Brownfield, Texas. Her father, Billy Swoopes, left shortly after her birth, leaving her mother, Louise, to raise her and her three brothers single-handedly. With only one income, the Swoopes household didn't always have a lot, but that didn't stop them from having fun.

One of the games the children often played together was basketball. Sheryl was interested in the sport at a very young age. Her brothers tried to keep her off the court at first, telling her she couldn't play with them because she was a girl. But Sheryl wouldn't give up. From the time she was seven, she showed up on the basketball court nearly every day after school to play with the boys.

Louise allowed Sheryl to play with her brothers but didn't really support her daughter's interest in the game. Reflecting on her mother's views later, Sheryl said:

❝When I was younger, she wanted me to go in the house and play with my dishes or my dolls. I guess it was just unheard of for a girl to play basketball, or she didn't want her little girl to get hurt.❞

Despite her mother's misgivings, Sheryl was allowed to pursue her interest. At age eight, she joined her first basketball team: the Little Dribblers. The experience was an eye-opener. She had never imagined that there were other little girls who wanted to play basketball too.

Sheryl continued to practice and grew better each year. By the time she reached high school, she was easily the best player on her team. After leading Brownfield High to the Texas State Championship in 1988, Sheryl was named Texas Player of the Year.

Louise eventually encouraged her daughter's love of basketball and attended all of Sheryl's home games. However, there was a strict "study first, basketball later" policy in effect in the Swoopes household. Although she didn't appreciate it at the time, Sheryl was grateful later for the good grades her mother's rule helped her achieve.

⇒ GOING TO COLLEGE ⇐

Because of her performance at Brownfield High, Sheryl was offered a **scholarship** to the University of Texas. The school's basketball team was one of the best in the country. Unfortunately, the University of Texas was 400 miles away from Sheryl's hometown. After only a few days into her first **semester**, Sheryl became so homesick that she decided to return to Brownsville and enroll in South Plains Junior College.

During her two years on the college's basketball team, Sheryl set 28 basketball records and was named National Junior College Player of the Year. In 1991 she transferred to Texas Tech University in nearby Lubbock. There, she played for the Lady Raiders and helped lead the team to two Southwest Conference titles in two seasons.

Martha Sharp, coach of the Lady Raiders, commented on Sheryl's ability after the team won back-to-back titles:

❝I can't tell you what Sheryl has meant to this program. She'll be a legend in women's basket-ball, but not just because of her play. She has a charisma that the crowd loves. You never doubt that she is a team player.❞

Sheryl transferred in 1991 from South Plains Junior College to Texas Tech, where she led the Lady Raiders to a 58-8 record in two seasons. Here, she cuts off the basketball net to celebrate the 84-82 win over Ohio State. The victory on April 5, 1993, earned Texas Tech the National Collegiate Athletic Association (NCAA) women's basketball championship title.

CROSS-CURRENTS

To learn about a unique opportunity that Cheryl received after graduating from college, check out "Air Swoopes." Go to page 50. ▶▶

The Texas Tech Lady Raiders won the NCAA Women's Basketball Championship in 1993. It was Sheryl's senior year. She scored a record-breaking 47 points in the title game against Ohio State. After the season, Sheryl was named National Player of the Year by nine organizations, including *Sports Illustrated* and *USA Today*.

⇒ A LEGEND WITHOUT A LEAGUE ⇐

Sheryl didn't have many opportunities to play basketball after college. She wasn't allowed to play in the National Basketball Association (NBA), and at the time there was no women's basketball league in the United States. Her only choice was to go overseas.

Although she didn't like the idea of not being able to play in her home country, Sheryl agreed to play in Italy for a team called the Basket Bari. She played 10 games in the fall of 1993 before quitting and returning to the States. This time she wasn't homesick. Sheryl felt that Basket Bari wasn't delivering on all of its promises. She has never explained what the contractual problems were, although she has said that the teams in Europe are paid by sponsors and getting paid can be tricky.

Back in Texas, Sheryl got a job as a bank teller and played in pickup games to stay in shape. In 1994 she joined Team USA, which represents the United States in international competitions. In July she played eight games in Sydney, Australia, and helped her team win a bronze medal in the world championships. The team went on to win a gold medal a month later in St. Petersburg, Russia, at the Goodwill Games.

CROSS-CURRENTS

Five Goodwill Games competitions were held between 1986 and 2001. To find out more, see "History of the Goodwill Games." Go to page 50. ▶▶

⇒ LIFE CHANGES ⇐

In February 1995 Sheryl made the U.S. team that would play in the Pan American Games. Unfortunately, the games were cancelled due to lack of interest. Out of options, Sheryl returned to Texas and her job as a bank teller.

Things began to turn around for Sheryl in May, when she secured one of 12 open spots on the women's Olympic team. The National Basketball Association (NBA) helped to schedule a nine-month tour

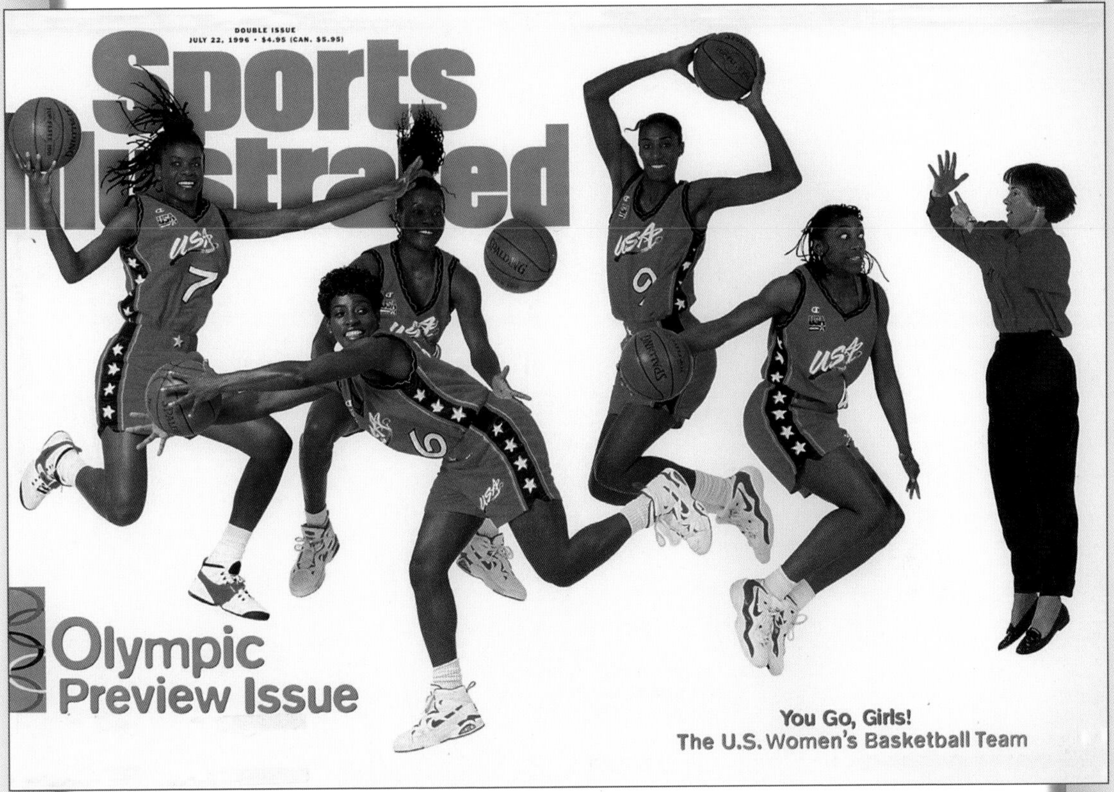

DOUBLE ISSUE
JULY 22, 1996 • $4.95 (CAN. $5.95)

Sports Illustrated

Olympic Preview Issue

You Go, Girls!
The U.S. Women's Basketball Team

Sports Illustrated Olympic Preview Issue features members of the U.S. women's basketball team on its July 22, 1996, cover. As a member of the team, Sheryl spent part of 1995 and 1996 participating in an exhibition-game tour held on four continents. Before leaving, she had married Eric Jackson and signed a sneakers endorsement contract with Nike.

so the team could practice by playing in exhibition games around the world. Right before she left for the tour, Sheryl married Eric Jackson, her high school sweetheart.

The U.S. team won all of its 52 exhibition games, then went on to win the gold medal at the 1996 Summer Olympics. The win was a huge accomplishment for Sheryl and the rest of the women on the team.

Sheryl Swoopes poses in her Houston Comets uniform. In October 1996 she became the first player signed by the Women's National Basketball Association, or WNBA. During the league's inaugural season, which began on June 21, 1997, there were eight teams: the Charlotte Sting, Cleveland Rockers, Houston Comets, New York Liberty, Los Angeles Sparks, Phoenix Mercury, Sacramento Monarchs, and Utah Starzz.

WNBA Champion

IN APRIL 1996 THE NBA ANNOUNCED ITS intention to sponsor a new professional women's basketball league known as the Women's National Basketball Association, or WNBA. The decision was monumental because it meant that Sheryl and other talented women like her would finally have the opportunity to play professional basketball on American soil.

On October 23, 1996, Sheryl signed the first WNBA contract. She was joined not long after by Olympic teammates Rebecca Lobo, Lisa Leslie, and Ruthie Bolton-Holifield. In the initial player allocation round of the 1997 WNBA drafts, the first 16 players were assigned to their teams at random. Sheryl was assigned to the Houston Comets, which meant that she got to stay in her home state of Texas.

CROSS-CURRENTS

If you'd like to learn more about this groundbreaking professional women's basketball league, read "History of the WNBA." Go to page 51. ▶▶

Like most of the other players, Sheryl was excited about the opportunities playing in the WNBA would provide. Shortly after signing her contract, she told the *New York Times*:

> **"I can't tell you how happy I am to be able to play professional basketball in the United States. It's like a dream come true for me. I've been around the NBA for a year now and I like the way they do things. I'm extremely excited to be associated with something like this."**

Right from the start, Sheryl was marketed as the league's top star. The WNBA needed her name and her talent to promote the idea of women's basketball. The league gave her a $150,000 personal service contract on top of the $50,000 the Houston Comets paid her, making her one of the three highest-paid women in the WNBA.

JORDAN ERIC JACKSON

Shortly after signing her new contract, Sheryl found out she was pregnant. The doctor told her she would be having her baby on June 21, 1997. As luck would have it, that was opening day of the first WNBA season.

Sheryl knew she would miss some of the first games and was nervous about the WNBA's reaction. At the same time, she was ready to have a child and excited about the prospect. Sheryl kept her secret to herself for a few months and continued to play pickup games to stay in shape. When she finally made the information public, the WNBA and her agent were very supportive. On June 25, 1997, Sheryl gave birth to Jordan Eric Jackson. The baby was named after his father, Eric Jackson, as well as basketball legend Michael Jordan.

CROSS-CURRENTS
To find out more about Michael Jordan, a basketball player Sheryl admires greatly, read "Sheryl's Role Model." Go to page 52. ▶▶

WNBA DEBUT

Not one to sit on the sidelines, Sheryl asked her doctor if she could start playing basketball just two days after Jordan was born. The doctor gave her permission to do so, and she immediately started training. She lifted weights, exercised, and got back out on the court to get back in shape and lose the 47 pounds she had gained while pregnant.

Michelle Timms, number seven for the Phoenix Mercury, watches as six-foot-tall shooting guard and forward Sheryl Swoopes of the Houston Comets goes for the basket. Timms would become known as a legendary player herself—the Australian woman was the WNBA's first international player. But in 1997 she, like many other players in the WNBA, regarded Sheryl as a formidable opponent.

Sheryl smiles during a July 1997 press conference, while Houston Comets coach Van Chancellor looks on. Because of the birth of her son, Jordan Eric Jackson, on June 25, Sheryl did not play with the Comets until August 7, toward the end of the WNBA inaugural season. However, she helped Houston win during the playoffs and ultimately secure the first WNBA championship title.

Forty-three days after giving birth, Sheryl made her first appearance as a **forward** in a WNBA game. The Houston fans gave her a standing ovation when she stepped out onto the court. After the game, WNBA commissioner Val Ackerman told reporters:

"The fact that she even attempted a comeback after having a baby is a testament to the kind of athlete she is. She has broken new ground for women's basketball."

Within a week, Sheryl was playing so well that it was hard to tell she had missed the first 19 games of the season. She played nine games in the regular season, finishing with averages of 7.1 points and 1.7 rebounds per game.

The Houston Comets made it to the playoffs that year and eventually faced off against the New York Liberty in the championship game. Sheryl still wasn't in top form at that point and was forced to watch most of the action from the bench. Despite her absence, the Comets played well and managed to win the 1997 WNBA Championship.

REBOUND

Sheryl knew she wasn't quite the athlete she had been before Jordan was born, so she worked hard to get back into the game. She wanted to be back in shape for the 1998 season. But she also had to take care of Jordan. Pulling double duty as a mom and a basketball star was one of the biggest challenges Sheryl faced. But she was determined, and she made it work.

By the time the Comets began practice in May 1998, Sheryl was at her pre-pregnancy weight of 145 pounds and as fast as ever. She turned down a chance to play in the World Championships for Team USA so that she could practice with her Houston teammates. The hard work paid off.

On June 11, during the first game of the season, Sheryl scored 28 points in only 27 minutes against the New York Liberty. The Comets won that game and 26 others by the end of the regular season. Going into the playoffs, they were clearly the team to beat.

BACK-TO-BACK CHAMPIONSHIPS

Sheryl had boosted her statistics to 15.6 points per game and 5.1 rebounds per game in the second WNBA season. She was named to the **All-WNBA team**, which meant she was one of the best players in the league. Her teammates Tina Thompson and Cynthia Cooper were named to the All-WNBA team, as well. Together, they became known as "The Big Three."

Sheryl and the Comets were the favorite to win the playoffs. Their first opponents in the opening round were the Charlotte Sting. Sheryl scored 17 points in the first game and had her first **double-double** in the second. The Comets won the first two games, making a third game unnecessary. The wins also meant that the Comets would play in the championship game once again. Their opponents would be the Phoenix Mercury.

The Mercury, which had some of the best players in the league, had been one of the few teams to beat the Comets during the regular season. Going into the first game, the Comets were confident. But they quickly lost their stride. Sheryl and her team members began having problems making their shots, and the Comets lost the game, 54-51.

The second and third games went much better for Houston. Sheryl made a significant contribution to the final point totals in both and helped lead her team to back-to-back wins over Phoenix. The victories gave the Comets their second consecutive WNBA Championship.

⇒ GIVING BACK ⇐

Sheryl made more money in 1998 than any other female athlete who played a team sport. She had endorsements with companies like Kellogg's and Discover Card and made money through licensing agreements with Nike, Hasbro, and other industry giants. The products Sheryl promoted included Air Swoopes, Swoopes jerseys, Swoopes basketballs, Swoopes action figures, and Swoopes trading cards. In 1998 her earnings were an estimated $1.2 million.

To give back, Sheryl did a lot of charity work. She was a spokesperson to raise awareness for RSV, a respiratory virus that affects babies and small children. She also donated money to her two favorite charities, the March of Dimes and UNICEF. In April 1999 she put on a milk-mustache with WNBA stars Lisa Leslie and Nikki McCray to support the Got Milk campaign and encourage good nutrition for children.

⇒ WNBA ALL-STAR ⇐

At the beginning of the 1999 basketball season, Sheryl announced she was divorcing her husband, Eric. Their marriage had fallen apart after their son was born, and they were unable to work out their differences. The divorce was tough on Sheryl, but she tried to remain positive and stay focused. In June she told reporters:

Sheryl drives to the basket during a game against the Detroit Shock. The Detroit WNBA team was one of the league's first expansion franchises, debuting in 1998. Its players had trouble stopping Sheryl Swoopes, who in 1998 was averaging 15 points per game. In 1999, she got even better, and averaged 18.3 points per game.

SHERYL SWOOPES

One of the off-the-court activities that Sheryl has participated in is serving as advisor to a Hewlett-Packard (HP) Web site designed for young people. The HP Digital Book Club featured links to reading and writing sites, recommended book lists, and writing tips from authors. This 1998 photo shows Sheryl attending a Digital Book club event at a bookstore in New York City.

"My whole thing is I don't want people to look at this as a negative. I think any time you go through something like this, it's going to be hard mentally, but I'm dealing with it. If I don't let the situation . . . distract me too much, I think this is going to be one of my best years."

As it turned out, 1999 was the year Sheryl truly broke out as a WNBA star. At the end of the season, she was ranked third in the league in scoring and had earned All-WNBA First Team honors. She averaged 18.3 points per game and led the Comets in steals and blocks. Sheryl also made WNBA history with the league's first **triple-double** when she racked up 14 points, 15 rebounds, and 10 assists playing against the Detroit Shock on July 27.

In 1999 Sheryl tried to stay positive when she talked with reporters about the divorce proceedings that would end her four-year marriage to her son's father, Eric Jackson. During one interview, she explained, "I'm just trying to stay focused and do what I have to do on the court because this is my job."

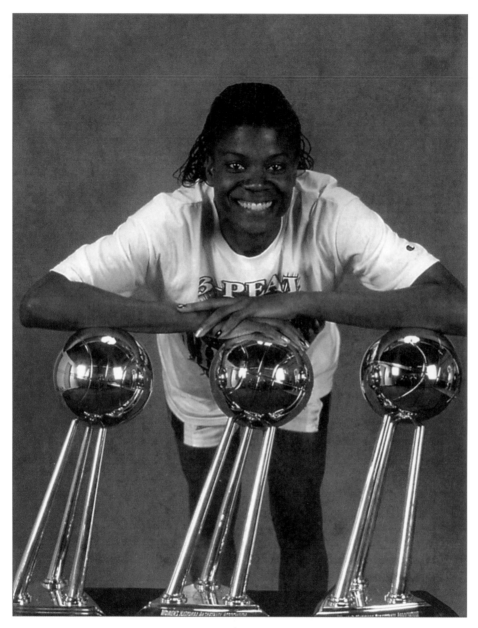

Sporting a "3-peat" T-shirt, Sheryl leans on the three WNBA championship trophies she helped the Houston Comets earn in 1997, 1998, and 1999. In 2000 she would help the team bring home a fourth WNBA championship title. That year she would earn the league's MVP for herself and lead the WNBA in scoring.

When the league announced it would hold the first WNBA All-Star game, basketball fans let everyone know who their favorite player was. Sheryl collected more votes than any other WNBA player and was named starting forward on the Western Conference team. On July 14, 1999, at the WNBA All-Star Game in New York City, she helped lead the team to a win against the Eastern Conference team. And after the end of the regular season, she helped lead the Comets to their third consecutive WNBA Championship.

⇒ LEAGUE MVP ⇐

Sheryl started the year 2000 with a new lease on life. Her divorce was behind her, and she was having more fun than ever on the court. It made a huge difference in her game. Although she had always been a **formidable** player, Sheryl suddenly seemed unstoppable.

She became the "go-to" player for the Comets and consistently scored more points than anyone else on her team. Her season average was 20.7 points per game, the best in the WNBA. She also led the league in steals, averaging 2.81 per game. At the end of the regular season, Sheryl was named the WNBA Player of the Year and Defensive Player of the Year.

The Comets went to the playoffs and easily advanced to the finals. For the third time in four years, their opponents were the New York Liberty. The Liberty were desperate to win a WNBA Championship, but Sheryl and the Comets prevailed again, winning their fourth straight title.

⇒ SYDNEY GAMES ⇐

Sheryl was named to the 2000 U.S. Women's Olympic Basketball Team at the end of June. When the WNBA season ended in August, she rushed to join her team in Australia to prepare for the Sydney Games. The team had won gold at the Atlanta Games in 1996, and everyone was hoping for a repeat performance.

On September 30, in the final game, the United States faced off against Australia. Both teams played hard, but the Australians were no match. Sheryl and her teammates executed a near-perfect game, winning 76-54, to secure their second consecutive gold medal.

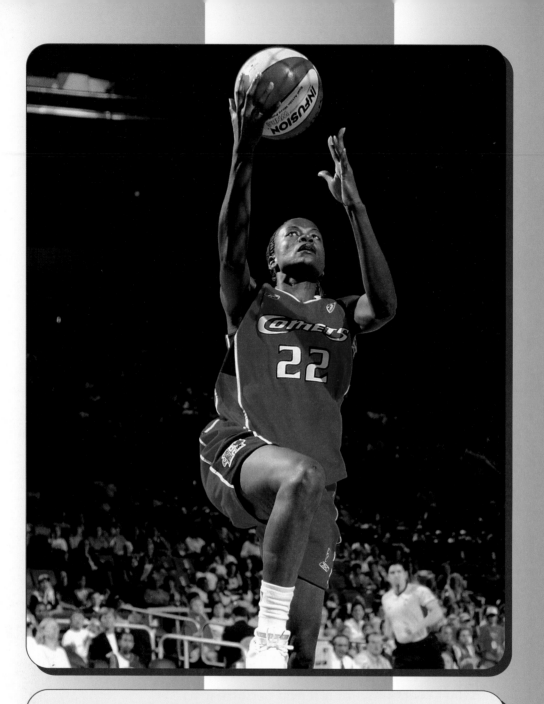

Sheryl Swoopes takes the ball to the basket. Despite a serious preseason injury in 2001, the Houston Comets star player wasn't about to give up. After taking the season off to recover and rehabilitate her knee, the queen of the courts would come back in 2002 and show herself worthy of the crown.

Queen of the Court

THE HOUSTON COMETS MADE HISTORY IN 2000 by winning their fourth straight WNBA championship. Only four professional sports teams—the Boston Celtics, Montreal Canadiens, New York Islanders, and New York Yankees—had ever been able to win four consecutive titles. Everyone was wondering if the Comets would be able to win a fifth title in 2001.

The team began training in early spring. During a preseason practice on April 23, Sheryl tore the **anterior cruciate ligament** and **lateral meniscus** in her left knee while running on the court. Her teammates told reporters she was going for a basket when she just collapsed on the floor in pain.

Sheryl and the Comets were devastated when they learned she would need surgery to fix her knee. The team's physician, Dr. Walter Lowe, said the injury was serious and would need time to heal. In a press conference, he told reporters:

> **"There is no magic dust. There is no question it will take longer than this season, but we expect her to be back next season."**

Sheryl underwent successful surgery in May to repair the injury. The Comets played well in the 2001 season without her, but weren't able to make it through the playoffs. In September 2001, the WNBA had a new championship team: the Los Angeles Sparks.

⟫ BOUNCING BACK ⟪

Coming back from such a severe injury was a brutal experience for Sheryl. She had a lot of pain to deal with and had to undergo months of **rehab**. At times, a full recovery seemed impossible. But she kept at it, working for two to three hours every day with the help of a personal trainer.

When she wasn't in rehab, Sheryl worked as a guest analyst for ESPN, the cable sports network. She also collaborated with author and photographer Susan Kuklin on a children's book called *Hoops with Swoopes*. The book showcased photographs of Sheryl playing basketball. *Hoops with Swoopes* won the Parent's Guide to Children's Media Award in 2001. On her Web site, Susan Kuklin wrote:

> **"It was exciting to learn a new way to show movement with still photography. But the best part about making this book was, I got to shoot hoops with Swoopes."**

⟫ BETTER THAN EVER ⟪

When the 2002 basketball season began, everyone was curious to see whether or not Sheryl was going to be able to make a comeback in the WNBA. A torn anterior cruciate ligament can be a career-ending injury. Athletes who are able to come back sometimes need two or more years to heal.

Sheryl was named to the USA World Championship Team in January. And when she returned to the Comets in early spring, she surprised everyone in the WNBA. Sheryl was playing better than ever. She scored 15 points in her first game of the season against the Los Angeles Sparks and didn't appear to be having any trouble with her

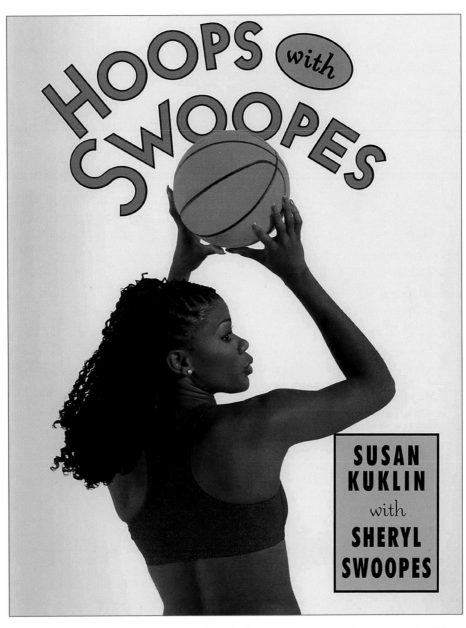

Hoops with Swoopes is a book for young readers created by Sheryl in collaboration with author and photographer Susan Kuklin. Published in May 2001, the book uses photographs of Sheryl in action to explain the basics of the game. Sheryl had previously coauthored a life's lessons book for kids called *Bounce Back,* based on her own experiences.

During a home game, Sheryl drives past Lisa Leslie of the Los Angeles Sparks. Although she was coming back from a serious injury, Sheryl played so well in 2002 that she earned two important honors: That August she was named a WNBA Most Valuable Player and WNBA Defensive Player of the Year.

knee. In reality, she did not feel 100 percent, but she was playing so well that it was impossible to tell.

In 14 games, Sheryl scored 20 points or more and ended the season with an average of 18.5 points per game, 4.9 rebounds per game, and 3.3 assists per game. She also played more minutes than any of her teammates and set a team record for most steals in a season. With Sheryl back on the team, the Comets were able to make it into the playoffs once again.

⟫ A SPECIAL HONOR ⟪

At the end of the 2002 season, Sheryl earned All-WNBA First Team honors. She was also named the WNBA's Most Valuable Player (**MVP**) and WNBA Defensive Player of the Year. It was the second time in three years that she had won both awards. At a special MVP ceremony held during the playoffs, WNBA president Val Ackerman commented on Sheryl's ability and her amazing comeback:

> **"**Sheryl is . . . a complete package. She's an extraordinary basketball player . . . the kind of player you count on to make a big play, she's the kind of player who lifts her teammates up . . . and she's the kind of player who knows what it takes to win . . . and this is what the Most Valuable Player of the WNBA is all about.**"**

CROSS-CURRENTS

To find out about other players who have been named the league's Most Valuable Player, read "MVPs of the WNBA." Go to page 53. ▶▶

Naturally, Sheryl was thrilled to be named MVP and Defensive Player of the Year. She said that she had never expected to return and play as well as she had. When she accepted her awards at the ceremony, she took time to thank everyone who helped her with her recovery and explained why each honor meant so much to her:

> **"**Never did I think I'd be able to come back this season and accomplish the things I've accomplished in such a short amount of time. Being named Defensive Player of the Year is no less an award than Most Valuable . . . so these are two very responsible and very special honors for me.**"**

⇛ READY TO WIN ⇚

Sheryl was happy to receive recognition for her performance, but what she really wanted to do was lead her team to another WNBA Championship. The Comets hadn't been able to win the title during her absence the previous year, and she desperately wanted to make up for the time she missed.

Unfortunately, things didn't work out quite the way Sheryl had hoped, as the Utah Starzz eliminated the Comets from the 2002 WNBA playoffs. Sheryl led her team in scoring in each of the three playoff games they played. She scored 28 points in two different games, but her effort still wasn't enough to beat the Starzz.

⇛ FIBA WORLD CHAMPIONSHIP ⇚

Sheryl didn't have much time to dwell on the Comets' loss. She joined the USA Basketball Women's World Championship Team almost immediately after the WNBA season ended. The team was scheduled to play in the Opals World Challenge in early September to warm up for the FIBA World Championship.

CROSS-CURRENTS

If you'd like some background history about an important international competition, read "FIBA World Championship for Women." Go to page 54. ▶▶

The Opals World Challenge, held in Newcastle and Homebush Bay, Australia, brought together the Australian, Brazilian, French, and American Olympic teams. This meant some of the best teams in the world were competing in the tournament, but the United States went undefeated through four games to win the championship. Sheryl averaged 15.5 points per game and won MVP honors.

After winning in Australia, the team went straight to the FIBA World Championship, in China. Sixteen teams were competing for the title. The United States beat team after team to eventually face off against Russia in the final games.

Sheryl and her team dominated the Russians in the first game, winning 89-55. The second game was a bit closer, but the U.S. women were able to eke out a 79-74 victory. The win gave the Americans their seventh gold medal, making them the leader in international play.

⇛ ANOTHER SUCCESSFUL YEAR ⇚

Sheryl rested for a few months after the World Championship before joining up with the Houston Stealth of the National Women's

In April 2003 Sheryl re-signed with the Houston Comets for a five-year-contract. At this point she had a career average of 17.6 points, 5.4 rebounds, and 2.5 steals per game. An ESPN story noted, "There aren't many players who are quicker with the basketball than she is. She's clutch, very deceptive and incredibly intelligent at both ends of the floor."

Basketball League (NWBL). This was a league for women that had been created in the mid-1990s. It played games in the fall and winter months—the WNBA off-season. Sheryl played 13 games for the Stealth during the NWBL season and helped lead the team to a NWBL Pro Cup victory.

The following April, Sheryl rejoined the Houston Comets. Throughout the 2003 season, Sheryl suffered several injuries, including a sprained ankle, a concussion, and bone spurs in her toe.

Nevertheless, she was able to score in the double digits 27 times in 31 games. She averaged 15.6 points per game for the season and led the league in steals. For the third time, Sheryl was voted WNBA Defensive Player of the Year.

Sheryl's performance helped the Comets make it into the WNBA playoffs for the seventh year in a row. However, they were eliminated in the first round by the Sacramento Monarchs.

⟫ A NEW SEASON ⟪

After three years of being eliminated in the playoffs the Comets were anxious to regain their championship standing in 2004. They hit the

The 2004 WNBA West Conference All-Stars. The best players of the WNBA East and West Conferences compete each July in the WNBA All-Star Game. In 2004 the WNBA took a month break so its players could participate in the Olympics. No All-Star game took place; however, the U.S. Olympic Team played a team of WNBA All-Stars at an exhibition game.

court with a vengeance but stumbled throughout the season. The team had its worst streak toward the end of the season, losing the last 10 games on the road.

In all, the Comets lost 21 of the 34 games they played and finished sixth in the WNBA Western Conference. It was the worst season they ever had and the first time in league history that Houston did not make it into the playoffs. Sheryl ended the season with an average of 14.8 points per game and 4.9 rebounds per game.

⇒ ATHENS GAMES ⇐

In August, after the end of the WNBA season, Sheryl joined the rest of the U.S. Olympic Women's Basketball Team for the 2004 Athens Games. The team was looking for a third consecutive Olympic gold medal. Some basketball observers questioned whether or not the American team would be able to accomplish its goal. Many of the women played for the WNBA, which meant that the 12-member squad had not had a chance to play together all year.

The team had only 13 days to prepare for the games, but somehow they managed. Its members won their first game against New Zealand on August 14, before systematically eliminating the competition to face off against Australia for the title. The U.S. team defeated the Australian team 74-63. It was a historic win for the team and for Sheryl, who now had her third Olympic gold medal. Only two other women in basketball had ever won gold three times in a row: her teammates Lisa Leslie and Dawn Staley.

⇒ COMMUNITY CONTRIBUTIONS ⇐

Although Sheryl is most well known for her basketball skills, she has also made many contributions to the community. She is very dedicated to causes that involve education and underprivileged children. In addition to participating in basketball camps through the NBA and other organizations, she has served on the advisory board of MADD (Mothers Against Drunk Driving) and worked with the WNBA in various programs.

Sheryl has also used her celebrity to form the Sheryl Swoopes Foundation for Youth. The organization is dedicated to educating young people and helping battered women and children around the world. Sheryl has donated both her time and money to maintain the foundation's activities.

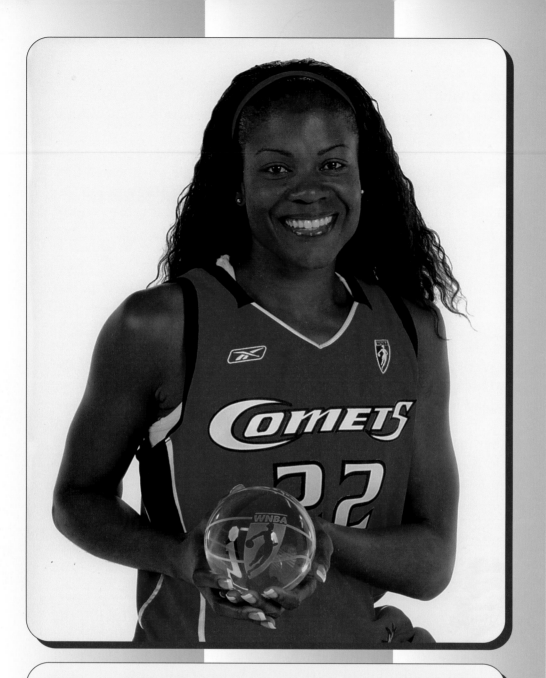

Superstar athlete Sheryl Swoopes shows off her 2005 WNBA Most Valuable Player trophy. During the course of her career she has been named the league's MVP three times (2000, 2002, and 2005). She has also been honored as the WNBA Defensive Player of the Year three times (2000, 2002 and 2003) and holds three Olympic gold medals and four WNBA championship titles.

Basketball Legend

THERE ARE MANY PLAYERS IN THE WNBA WHO are famous, but there are very few who have been superstars since the league began in 1997. As 34-year-old Sheryl Swoopes began her ninth season with the WNBA, she was still with the Houston Comets. And she would soon show that she was still one of the best players in the league.

Sheryl had a fantastic season in 2005. She led the WNBA in scoring, averaging 18.6 points per game, and was second in steals. In August she set two career highs when she scored 34 points against Seattle and then nabbed 12 offensive rebounds when playing Phoenix.

As usual, Sheryl was instrumental in leading her team to the playoffs. She was named the WNBA MVP for the third time and received All-WNBA First Team honors and All-Defensive First Team honors. She was also the MVP of the WNBA All-Star Game.

In game three of the semifinals, Sheryl recorded the first triple-double in WNBA playoff history and finished the game with 14 points, 10 assists, and 10 rebounds. The Comets performed well enough to reach the Western Conference finals. But Sheryl and her team lost to the Sacramento Monarchs.

THE *ESPN* INTERVIEW

When the 2005 basketball season ended, Sheryl surprised the world when she told *ESPN The Magazine* that she was gay. She had fallen in love with Alisa Scott, a former basketball player and assistant coach of the Houston Comets. Sheryl had kept the relationship a secret for seven years, since a year before her divorce, and couldn't stand to hide it any longer. She told *ESPN*:

> **"I'm tired of having to hide my feelings about . . . the person I love. Some people might say my coming out after just winning the MVP Award is heroic, and . . . I know there are going to be some negative things said, too. But it doesn't change who I am. I can't help who I fall in love with. No one can."**

Because she was the first well-known WNBA athlete to declare she was gay, Sheryl was worried that some of the fans and league members might be hostile towards her. But her worries were for nothing. Fans gave her a standing ovation the next time she appeared on the court, and the Houston Comets didn't treat her any differently. Van Chancellor, the head coach of the Comets since 1997, released the following statement the day after Sheryl's announcement:

> **"I've coached Sheryl Swoopes for nine years with the Houston Comets, as well as with the national team. What she does in her personal life is her own decision. I respect everything about Sheryl, how she's handled herself on and off the court. To me, she will always be one of the greatest ambassadors for the game of women's basketball."**

According to Sheryl, the WNBA itself had a different reaction to the news. While there was no official statement regarding her

Sheryl with partner Alisa Scott. In October 2005, one month after receiving her third MVP, Sheryl told *ESPN The Magazine* that she was gay. "Being gay has nothing to do with the three gold medals or the three MVPs or the four championships I've won. I'm still the same person. I'm Sheryl," she stated.

announcement, Sheryl has noted that she believes the league no longer markets her as aggressively as it once did.

⟫ A FINANCE LESSON ⟪

Sheryl felt better after revealing her secret, but she still had other problems to work through. One of her largest problems involved money. Sheryl was one of the highest-paid players in the WNBA, but she had been spending more than she was making for the past few years. In late October 2005, she admitted to reporters that she was struggling with debt and had to file bankruptcy the previous year. She told the *New York Times*:

> **"Growing up not having a lot of money, I was suddenly in a position to change my lifestyle and help those around me. But I didn't surround myself with the right people. I got in a position where it was like, 'Oh, wow, what happened?'"**

Sheryl blamed some of her money troubles on a bad accountant, but said that a lot of the problem was simple overspending. Sheryl knew she had made mistakes and was taking steps to pay back her creditors. In talking about her problems with debt, she hoped to inspire other athletes to be more responsible with their money.

SEASON NUMBER TEN

Going into her tenth season as a WNBA player, Sheryl was still on top of her game in 2006. She was one of the leading scorers in the league and one of the top defensive players. Her season averages were 15.5 points, 5.9 rebounds, and 3.7 assists per game.

Sheryl also played in the WNBA All-Star Game before helping to lead the Comets to the playoffs yet again. Unfortunately, the Comets couldn't get past the Sacramento Monarchs in the 2006 semifinals. The Monarchs went on to win the WNBA Championship for the second year in a row.

VALIDATION

Sheryl was awarded a great honor in 2006 when she was named to the National Collegiate Athletic Association's 25th Anniversary Team. She was selected by college administrators, basketball coaches, and representatives of the Women's Basketball Hall of Fame based on her stellar performance in the NCAA tournament in 1993. The award validated what everyone already knew: Sheryl was one of the greatest college basketball players of all time.

Later in the year, Sheryl was also named to the WNBA's All-Decade Team. The team included the 10 best and most influential players from the league's first 10 years of play. Sheryl was one of 30 nominees voted in by fans, a media panel, and WNBA players and coaches. When the announcement was made, WNBA president Donna Orender released a statement that read:

> **"The All-Decade Team represents the very best in women's professional basketball. . . . The group consists of not only tremendous athletes who have reached extraordinary heights on the court, but of terrific women who give unselfishly of their time and effort in the community. They are multi-faceted role models, believers, dreamers, achievers, coaches, teachers, leaders and champions."**

Sheryl drives the ball through three Seattle Storm defenders during a game in 2006. That year the WNBA announced that four Houston Comets players had been named to the league's All-Decade Team. Retired player Cynthia Cooper, along with active players Dawn Staley, Sheryl Swoopes, and Tina Thompson were voted by their fans, peers, and the media to the team.

➤ ANOTHER TEAM SUCCESS ◆

Sheryl continued to play on the USA Basketball Women's Senior National Team as it experienced many successes from 1996 to 2005. It had a 42-0 winning streak that has never been paralleled in women's sports. During the 10-year period, the team won five consecutive medals at the FIBA World Championships and the Olympic Games.

In 2006 the women's team was hoping to add another FIBA World Championship title to its record. Members of the team began practicing together in the spring to prepare for the World Championship that would take place in September in Brazil. Since many of the players participated in the WNBA as well, some members of the team got more practice than others.

Still, the U.S. team was able to do very well against the other 14 national teams that competed. It won all three games in the preliminaries and the quarterfinals before losing to the Russian team in the semifinals. The United States was still able to take home a bronze medal, though, after beating Brazil 99-59 in the medal finals.

➤ OUT FOR THE SEASON ◆

Three games into the 2007 WNBA season Sheryl suffered another injury. This time it wasn't an ankle or her knee; it was her back. She was evaluated and then diagnosed with a bulging disc. Initially, doctors thought Sheryl would be out for two to four weeks at the most. However, it quickly became evident that the injury was worse than they thought.

Sheryl was forced to have back surgery in September to remove the disc between her third and fourth **lumbar vertebrae**. It is a painful procedure that can be tough to recover from, but Sheryl was committed to getting better. The thought of retiring because of an injury was just too heartbreaking for her to consider. She always had the goal of retiring when she was still playing at her best.

➤ SPREADING A MESSAGE OF HOPE ◆

Sheryl has been a motivational speaker at many different events throughout her career. While she was recovering from her surgery in 2008, she continued to spread her message of hope at various engagements. One of her favorite topics to discuss is success. On February 19, 2008, she encouraged a crowd at the University of Missouri in Kansas City to make the best of unpleasant situations:

"Adversity can sometimes be one of the better things that can happen to a person. It provides time for reflection . . . it creates a new sense of purpose, it builds character and it will also motivate and challenge you to excel. . . . In the end, it's what you take from . . . your adverse situation to turn a negative to a positive . . . to create a better future."

Sheryl waves to crowd during a March 2, 2007, parade at Disneyland, in Anaheim, California. The celebration was part of ESPN The Weekend at Disney-MGM Studios (now known as Disney's Hollywood Studios). Held annually, the event is a sports-themed fan-fest that features live ESPN telecasts and motorcade parades of famous athletes.

SHERYL SWOOPES

At the Human Rights Campaign (HRC) 11th Annual National Dinner, Sheryl accepts the National Visibility Award from Black Entertainment Television (B.E.T.) cofounder Sheila Johnson. At the event, which took place in October 2007, at the Washington, D.C., Convention Center, Swoopes was honored for being open and honest about her sexual identity.

Sheryl speaks from experience. She has overcome adversity time and time again in her life and in her career. The problems she has faced include financial woes, divorce, and career-threatening injuries. But Sheryl has managed to rise above it all and become one of the most accomplished basketball players in history.

⋙ WHAT THE FUTURE HOLDS ⋘

After 11 years with the Houston Comets, Sheryl decided not to return to the team following her back surgery. She instead opted to sign a multiyear contract with the Seattle Storm on March 3, 2008. The exact length of the contract was not disclosed, but Sheryl is guaranteed to play at least one year in a Storm uniform.

Now that Sheryl has recovered from her back surgery, she is looking forward to playing basketball for another few seasons before retiring. She also wants to do more work through basketball camps and her charitable organization, the Sheryl Swoopes Foundation for Youth. There is also a chance that Sheryl will explore sports broadcasting after retirement. For many years now, she has said that she is interested in securing a job as a broadcast journalist or sports commentator.

Whatever Sheryl decides to do in the future, she will always be remembered for the amazing contributions she has made to basketball and to the community. She was the first woman in the WNBA, and she helped put women's basketball on the map. She is and always will be a modern hero on and off the court.

CROSS-CURRENTS

To learn how Sheryl may use her speaking ability after her playing days are over, read "Sports Broadcasting." Go to page 54. ▶▶

CROSS-CURRENTS

For some history about Sheryl's new WNBA team, check out the short article "The Seattle Storm." Go to page 55. ▶▶

Women's Basketball in the Olympics

Women's basketball made its debut at the Olympic Games in 1976. That year, the team from the Soviet Union defeated the United States in the finals to win the gold medal. The U.S. team finished with the silver medal, while a team from Bulgaria took the bronze.

The Soviet team won again in 1980, this time easily defeating Bulgaria 104 to 73 for the gold medal. The U.S. team did not participate in the Games that year, which were held in the Soviet capital of Moscow. The United States was boycotting the Summer Olympics to protest the Soviet invasion of Afghanistan in 1979.

During the 1980s, the American Olympic basketball teams featured such talented players as Cheryl Miller and Anne Donovan. Both were great players in college who never had an opportunity to play professionally in the United States because there was no women's basketball league. Thanks to their efforts, the United States won Olympic gold medals in 1984 (the Soviets did not compete) and 1988.

Before the 1992 Olympics began, the Soviet Union collapsed, breaking into many smaller countries. Athletes from these former Soviet states competed together as the Unified Team in 1992 and beat China to win the gold. The U.S. team finished third. The United States then came back to win gold medals at the 1996, 2000, and 2004 Olympic Games. (Go back to page 6.) ◄◄

Sheryl's Olympic Teammates

Sheryl has played with Lisa Leslie and Dawn Staley in three different Olympic Games. Together, these three women led the U.S. Women's Olympic Basketball Team to three consecutive gold medals.

Lisa Leslie was one of the first women to sign with the WNBA and still plays with the Los Angeles Sparks. In 2001 and 2002, she led the Sparks to back-to-back WNBA championships. Among other things, Lisa is known for her scoring and dunking ability. She is the top U.S. Olympic scorer ever, with a total of 407 points in the 1996, 2000, and 2004 Games. In 2002 she became the first woman in the WNBA to dunk during a game.

Dawn Staley has enjoyed success as both a player and a coach. In her four years at the University of Virginia, she led her team to three NCAA **Final Four** appearances. After graduating, Dawn played basketball in France, Italy, Brazil, and Spain before joining the now defunct American Basketball League. She was drafted into the WNBA in 1999 and helped lead the Charlotte Sting to the 2001 WNBA Championship game. She retired from the WNBA at the end of the 2005 season. Staley is currently the coach of the women's basketball team at Temple University, a job she has held since 1999.

Wearing USA number 9, Lisa Leslie battles her Ukrainian opponent during a preliminary round of the 1996 Olympics, held in July, in Atlanta, Georgia. The success of Team USA in Atlanta helped create interest in a women's pro league. Lisa joined one of the original eight WNBA teams, the Los Angeles Sparks in 1997, and still plays for the team today. (Go back to page 9.) ◀◀

Air Swoopes

In the mid-1980s, Air Jordan shoes—named after basketball star Michael Jordan—helped make Nike, Inc., one of the most successful sportswear companies in the world. In 1993 Nike decided to introduce a women's basketball shoe similar to the Air Jordan to attract more female athletes. The company turned immediately to Sheryl Swoopes, who was already being paid to wear its apparel and make special appearances.

Although Sheryl thought Nike was joking at first, she readily agreed to the deal. She was a new college graduate and fresh off her win at the NCAA Women's Basketball Championship. But with no league to play for, she had to rely on her income from her job as a bank teller. A Nike **endorsement** would change that.

After getting input from Sheryl, designers began drawing the shoe in 1994. By 1995 the shoe was ready for the market. Nike introduced Air Swoopes at a New York press conference on March 29. The shoes were sold out as soon as they hit shelves.

It was a historic moment for Sheryl and for women's sports. Up until that point, no female athlete had ever had a shoe named after her. To this day, Sheryl is credited with breaking the glass ceiling in sports marketing.

(Go back to page 14.) ◀◀

History of the Goodwill Games

In 1980 the United States and several other countries boycotted the Olympic Games in Moscow because the Soviets had invaded Afghanistan. In response, the Soviet Union and other Eastern European countries refused to attend the 1984 Olympics in Los Angeles. To help ease tensions between the two countries, media mogul and philanthropist Ted Turner decided to create the Goodwill Games as an alternative to the Olympics.

The first Goodwill Games were held in Moscow in 1986. More than 3,000 athletes representing 79 countries showed up to compete in 182 events. Like the Olympics, the Goodwill Games were scheduled to take place every four years, with the location alternating between the Soviet Union and the United States. Even after the Soviet Union broke apart in the early 1990s, the games continued.

In 1998 Turner sold the rights to the Goodwill Games to TimeWarner. That corporation organized a winter version of the games in 2000 and a summer game in 2001, but the events were relatively small. With the Soviet Union gone, there was less need for a competition designed to bring people together. TimeWarner decided to eliminate the competition. Although the Goodwill Games no longer exist, the athletes who participated and the fans who watched will always remember the friendships that were formed in the midst of the Cold War. (Go back to page 14.) ◀◀

History of the WNBA

The NBA Board of Governors announced the formation of the Women's National Basketball Association (WNBA) at a press conference on April 24, 1996. Six months later, the league began signing the first players to the eight teams that would compete in the **inaugural** season. Many of the players were Olympians and college stars.

The WNBA's first marketing campaign used the slogan "We Got Next" and the league's best-known players to promote games. Sheryl Swoopes, Lisa Leslie, and Rebecca Lobo all appeared in WNBA advertisements that featured the slogan.

The first WNBA game was played by the New York Liberty and Los Angeles Sparks on June 21, 1997, at the Great Western Forum in Los Angeles. The game was televised by the NBC network. The teams played in front of 14,284 fans, and the televised game garnered a 3.8 Nielsen rating, higher than any other national sports competition that evening.

The WNBA has lasted longer than any other team-oriented professional sports league for women. Since its debut, the league has grown into a home for some of the best basketball players in the world. The WNBA has also made an effort

Rebecca Lobo (left) and Sheryl Swoopes were both signed by the WNBA in October 1996. The following January the fledgling league assigned Lobo to the New York Liberty. She played with the WNBA from 1997 to 2003, before retiring due to injuries. Today she is a sports analyst and commentator focusing on women's college basketball games and WNBA games.

to give back to the community and the fans through outreach initiatives like the Jr. WNBA and the WNBA Read to Achieve program.

(Go back to page 17.) ◀◀

Sheryl's Role Model

Sheryl has stated on numerous occasions that Michael Jordan is one of her role models. As a young player, she looked up to him, and later in life she named her son after him. Sheryl has even been called the "female Michael Jordan."

One of the greatest basketball players of all time, Michael Jordan played professional basketball between 1984 and 2003. He was the superstar of the NBA league and possibly the most marketed athlete in history, from any sport. Nike's Air Jordan sneakers raked in millions of dollars and left a permanent mark on pop culture.

Michael played for the University of Carolina before joining the NBA's Chicago Bulls in 1984. He went on to break nearly every NBA record imaginable and eventually led his team to six NBA Championships. In 1993 he surprised everyone by retiring from basketball and signing a

Basketball legend Michael Jordan. The star athlete designed and endorsed Nike sneakers known as Air Jordan, released in 1984. A little more than a decade later, Sheryl Swoopes had a Nike shoe bearing her name, the Air Swoopes. "That's the greatest compliment I've ever received," she told Sports Illustrated *in 1996, "because Michael has always been my idol."*

minor league baseball contract with the Chicago White Sox.

Less than a year later, he returned to play basketball for the Bulls. In 1999 Michael retired for the second time but couldn't stay off the court for long. He returned to the NBA and began playing for the Washington Wizards in 2001. Michael played his last professional basketball game in April of 2003 before retiring for the third and final time. He is now a businessman and philanthropist.

(Go back to page 18.) ◀◀

MVPs of the WNBA

Every year the WNBA honors one WNBA player with the Most Valuable Player (MVP) Award. This award is given to the player who was most valuable to her team during the regular basketball season. To keep it fair, an unbiased panel of broadcasters and sports writers cast votes for the players to determine who will win. The WNBA player that gets the most votes is awarded the MVP during the playoffs.

Winning the MVP is a significant achievement and a great honor for any player. Sheryl Swoopes won the WNBA's coveted MVP award three times. Cynthia Cooper, Lisa Leslie, and Lauren Jackson have also won the award multiple times. Only once, in 1997, did a player in the Eastern Conference win the MVP. At that time, the Houston Comets were part of the Eastern Conference.

Year	Player	Team
1997	Cynthia Cooper	Houston Comets
1998	Cynthia Cooper	Houston Comets
1999	Yolanda Griffith	Sacramento Monarchs
2000	Sheryl Swoopes	Houston Comets
2001	Lisa Leslie	Los Angeles Sparks
2002	Sheryl Swoopes	Houston Comets
2003	Lauren Jackson	Seattle Storm
2004	Lisa Leslie	Los Angeles Sparks
2005	Sheryl Swoopes	Houston Comets
2006	Lisa Leslie	Los Angeles Sparks
2007	Lauren Jackson	Seattle Storm

(Go back to page 33.) ◀◀

FIBA World Championship for Women

The International Basketball Federation (FIBA) is the governing body for basketball worldwide. This means that the organization is in charge of defining basketball rules and appointing referees for international games. Formed by 213 national federations of basketball throughout the world, FIBA controls every international competition that takes place, including the FIBA World Championship for Women and the FIBA World Championship for Men.

Also known as the Basketball World Championship for Women, the FIBA World Championship for Women is a basketball tournament that is held every four years. Sixteen national teams from all over the world compete in the tournament. Winning the FIBA World Championship is considered a great accomplishment—similar to winning an Olympic medal.

The FIBA World Championship for Women was first held in March 1953. In the history of the event, only four teams have ever won gold medals. The United States has won seven times, followed by the Soviet Union (six), Brazil (one), and Australia (one).

The U.S. women's team has dominated the competition in the past three decades, winning five out of eight World Championship titles. Its consistent performance makes the team the top-ranked basketball team in the world. (Go back to page 34.) ◀◀

Sports Broadcasting

Sheryl has said she would like to get a job in sports broadcasting after she retires from basketball. She is particularly interested in being a broadcast journalist or sports commentator. Here is what these jobs require:

A broadcast journalist focuses on sports and delivers sports-related news on the television, radio, and online. Like other journalists, sports journalists must sniff out a good story and find a way to make it interesting to the general public. Sports journalists must be able to speak clearly and effectively. They must also be able to demonstrate their knowledge of sports and be enthusiastic about the news they are reporting.

Also known as a sportscaster or announcer, a sports commentator comments on basketball games (or other types of games) as they are being played. Commentators are expected to be knowledgeable about the sport they are announcing and are expected to fill air time with interesting statistics. Sports commentators need many of the same skills required to become a broadcast journalist. They must be well-spoken and enthusiastic about the sport they are announcing. They also need in-depth knowledge of game rules and players. But unlike sports journalists, commentators do not do investigative reporting.

(Go back to page 47.) ◀◀

The Seattle Storm

In March 2008, Sheryl signed a contract to play for the Seattle Storm. Since entering the WNBA in 2000, the Storm has been one of the league's most successful franchises. The team made five playoff appearances in its first eight seasons, and won the WNBA Championship in 2004.

As a member of the Seattle Storm, Sheryl plays with other All-Stars like Lauren Jackson, Sue Bird, and Swin Cash. The coach of the Storm, Brian Agler, has coached two other professional women's basketball teams and has won two professional titles. Like the Houston Comets, the Seattle Storm competes in the Western Conference. As a Storm player, Sheryl faces off against many of the same teams that she has always played against, including the Phoenix Mercury and the Los Angeles Sparks.

At one time, the same investors owned both the Storm and the Seattle SuperSonics, an NBA franchise. However, because the ownership group intended to move the SuperSonics to another city, in February 2008 the Storm was sold to a group of Seattle investors called Force 10 Hoops, LLC. This meant that even if the Sonics moved, the Storm would continue to play in Seattle. (Go back to page 47.) ◀◀

WNBA Seattle Storm players warm up before a home game at the Key Arena, in Seattle, Washington. After 11 years with the Houston Comets, Sheryl joined the Storm in 2008. "My experiences and the success I've had in playing, I think I can bring that to this team," Swoopes has said.

1971   Sheryl Denise Swoopes is born March 25 in Brownfield, Texas.

1993   After leading Texas Tech University to the National Championship, Sheryl sets an NCAA record for points scored in a title game. She is named National Player of the Year by nine organizations, including *Sports Illustrated* and *USA Today*.

1995   Nike gives Sheryl a new endorsement deal and names a shoe after her.

1996   Sheryl wins the gold medal with the U.S. Women's Olympic Basketball Team at the Summer Olympics in Atlanta, Georgia.

1997   Son Jordan Eric Jackson is born on June 25. Sheryl makes her WNBA debut on August 7.

1999   Sheryl records the WNBA's first triple-double on July 27 with 14 points, 15 rebounds, and 10 assists. She helps lead her team to its third consecutive championship.

2000   Sheryl wins the gold medal with the U.S. Women's Olympic Basketball Team at the Summer Olympics in Sydney, Australia. She is named WNBA MVP and WNBA Defensive Player of the Year.

2001   After tearing the anterior cruciate ligament and lateral meniscus in her knee, Sheryl misses the 2001 season.

2002   Sheryl is named WNBA MVP and WNBA Defensive Player of the Year. She also helps her team win gold at the FIBA World Championship.

2003   For the second year in a row, Sheryl earns the WNBA Defensive Player of the Year Award. She is also inducted into the Texas Tech Hall of Fame.

2004   Sheryl wins the gold medal with the U.S. Women's Olympic Basketball Team at the Summer Olympics in Athens. She is inducted into the Texas Women's Hall of Fame by Texas governor Rick Perry.

2005   In addition to earning a place on the All-WNBA First Team and being selected All-Defensive First Team, Sheryl is named WNBA MVP for the third time.

2006   Sheryl earns the bronze medal with the USA Basketball Women's Senior National Team at the FIBA World Championship for Women in Brazil.

2007   Sheryl has back surgery to remove the disc between her third and fourth lumbar vertebrae. She misses all but the first three games of the 2007 WNBA season.

2008   After 11 years with the Houston Comets, Sheryl joins the Seattle Storm.

Awards

1991 NJCAA Player of the Year

1992 Southwest Conference Newcomer of the Year
Southwest Conference Player of the Year

1993 Associated Press Female Athlete of the Year
Babe Zaharias Female Athlete of the Year Award
Final Four's Most Outstanding Player
Naismith College Player of the Year
Southwest Conference Player of the Year
WBCA Player of the Year

1998 March of Dimes Sportswoman of the Year Award
All-WNBA First-Team

1999 All-WNBA First-Team

2000 All-WNBA First-Team
WNBA Defensive Player of the Year
WNBA Most Valuable Player

2001 ESPY Award for Women's Pro Basketball Player of the Year

2002 All-WNBA First-Team
Opals World Challenge MVP
WNBA Defensive Player of the Year
WNBA Most Valuable Player

2003 BET Female Athlete of the Year
WNBA Defensive Player of the Year

2005 All-Defensive First Team
All-Star MVP Award
All-WNBA First-Team
WNBA Most Valuable Player

2006 All-Decade Team
Spirit Award

2007 National Visibility Award

2008 World Pride & Power Lifetime Achievement Award

WNBA Career Season Averages

Year	Games Played	Field Goals (percentage)	Points Per Game	Rebounds Per Game
1997	9	0.472	7.1	1.7
1998	29	0.427	15.6	5.1
1999	32	0.462	18.3	6.3
2000	31	0.506	20.7	6.3
2002	32	0.434	18.5	4.9
2003	31	0.403	15.6	4.6
2004	31	0.422	14.8	4.9
2005	33	0.447	18.6	3.6
2006	31	0.413	15.5	5.9
2007	3	0.360	7.7	5.7
Career	262	0.441	16.8	5.1
All-Star	6	0.392	8.3	5.0

Books

Bandy, Lana. *The Ultimate Women's Basketball Trivia and Puzzle Book*. Terre Haute, Ind.: Wish Publishing, 2008.

Brock, Ted. *Ladies of the Court*. Mankato, Minn.: Child's World, 2007.

Burby, Liza N. *Sheryl Swoopes: All-Star Basketball Player*. New York: The Rosen Publishing Group, 2001.

Grundy, Pamela and Susan Shackelford. *Shattering the Glass: The Remarkable History of Women's Basketball*. Chapel Hill: The University of North Carolina Press, 2007.

Kuklin, Susan, and Sheryl Swoopes. *Hoops with Swoopes*. New York: Hyperion Books for Children, 2001.

Rappoport, Ken. *Sheryl Swoopes: Star Forward*. Berkeley Heights, N.J.: Enslow Publishers, 2002.

Terzieff, Juliette. *Women of the Court: Inside the WNBA*. New York: Alyson Books, 2008.

Web Sites

http://espn.go.com/

The ESPN Web site is dedicated to providing updates on all aspects of women's basketball. In addition to interviews with Sheryl, the site includes stats, photos, a blog, and much more.

http://www.usabasketball.com/

The official Web site of USA Basketball includes a calendar of events and information on USA basketball history, as well as interviews with Sheryl.

http://www.usolympicteam.com

The U.S. Olympic Team's official site has an entire web page devoted to Sheryl that includes quotes, stats, and other interesting information.

http://www.wnba.com

The official Web site of the WNBA features a player profile for Sheryl, game logs, and career statistics.

All-WNBA team—an annual honor awarded to the best players in the league following every WNBA season. The team consists of two forwards, two guards, and one center. Team members are chosen based on the number of votes they receive from members of the Associated Press.

anterior cruciate ligament—a major ligament, or connective tissue, in the knee. It connects the bones of the upper and lower leg.

assist—the act of passing the ball to another teammate in a play that results in her scoring.

double-double—the term used to describe when a player in a game gets a double-digit number in at least two categories: assists, blocked shots, points, rebounds, or steals.

endorsement—the act of recommending a product or service, often in exchange for money from an individual or organization.

exhibition games—practice games.

Final Four—four regional champions in the National Collegiate Athletic Association (NCAA) annual championship tournament.

formidable—impressive or awe inspiring.

forward—a player who positions herself to make baskets and get rebounds while on offense and defense. Many basketball teams have a small forward, who is responsible for scoring points, and a power forward, who is responsible for getting rebounds.

inaugural—the first or beginning.

lateral meniscus—a crescent-shaped wedge of cartilage in the outer edge of the knee joint.

lumbar vertebrae—bones that make up the spinal column in the lower back.

MVP—most valuable player.

pickup games—unorganized games played by individuals who "pick up" enough random players to make a temporary team.

playoffs—a series of games played to determine a championship.

rehab—rehabilitation; treatment to aid recovery from an injury or illness.

scholarship—money awarded to a student to help pay for the cost of education.

semester—half of a year of college.

triple-double—the term used to describe when a player in a game gets a double-digit number in at least three categories: assists, blocked shots, points, rebounds, or steals.

page 6 "I like to think . . ." USA Basketball, "Pioneers of American Domination" (2006). http://www.usabasketball.com/seniorwomen/2006/06_wsnt_95-96anniversary.html

page 7 "There are not many . . ." "Women's Olympic Team," *New York Times* (February 3, 2000). http://query.nytimes.com/gst/fullpage.html?res=9B00EEDB133FF930A35751C0A9669C8B63&sec=&spon=&pagewanted=2

page 9 "This third one . . ." U.S. Olympic Team, "Sheryl Swoopes Athlete Bio" (2004). http://www.usolympicteam.com/26_1156.htm

page 12 "When I was younger . . ." Erin Davies, "Heir Jordan" *Texas Monthly Biz* (June 1999), p. 30.

page 12 "I can't tell you . . ." Kelli Anderson, "Rhymes with Hoops" *Sports Illustrated* (April 12, 1993), p. 42.

page 18 "I can't tell you . . ." William C. Rhoden, "Women's W.B.A Takes First Big Step," *New York Times* (October 24, 1996). http://query.nytimes.com/gst/fullpage.html?res=940CE1DA1330F937A15753C1A960958260&scp=57&sq=sheryl+swoopes&st=nyt.

page 21 "The fact that she . . ." "Sheryl Swoopes: A Basketball Star Controls the Dribble at Home and on the Hardwood" *People Weekly* (December 29, 1997), p. 68.

page 24 "My whole thing is . . ." "Sheryl Swoopes, WNBA Star, Divorcing Husband" *Jet* (June 7, 1999), p. 50.

page 30 "There is no magic . . ." "Swoopes Will Miss Season" *New York Times* (April 25, 2001). http://query.nytimes.com/gst/fullpage.html?res=9D07EFD71739F936A 15757C0A9679C8B63&scp=153&sq=sheryl+swoopes&st=nyt

page 30 "It was exciting to . . ." Susan Kuklin, statement on Web site (2001). http://susankuklin.com/work5.htm

page 33 "Sheryl is . . ." Houston Comets, "Sheryl Swoopes Named 2002 WNBA MVP" (2002). http://www.wnba.com/comets/news/Sheryl_Swoopes_Named_2002_WNBA-51672-222.html

page 33 "Never did I think . . ." Houston Comets, "Sheryl Swoopes Named 2002 WNBA MVP."

page 40 "I'm tired of having . . ." Sheryl Swoopes, as told to LZ Granderson, "Outside the Arc" *ESPN The Magazine* (October 26, 2005). http://sports.espn.go.com/espn/print?id=2204322&type=story

page 40 "I've coached Sheryl Swoopes . . ." Liz Robbins, "Swoopes Says She Is Gay, and Exhales" *New York Times* (October 27, 2005). http://www.nytimes.com/2005/10/27/sports/basketball/27swoopes.html?scp=17&sq=sheryl+swoopes&st=nyt

page 42 "Growing up not having . . ." Robbins, "Swoopes Says She Is Gay, and Exhales."

page 43 "The All-Decade Team . . ." WNBA Press Release, "WNBA Announces All-Decade Team" (June 13, 2006). http://www.wnba.com/news/alldecaderelease_060613.html

page 45 "Adversity can sometimes be . . ." David Cordill, "Basketball Champ Speaks About Coming Out, Success" University News Web site (February 25, 2008). http://media.www.unews.com/media/storage/paper274/news/2008/02/25/Culture/Basketball.Champ.Speaks.About.Coming.Out.Success-3232931.shtml

---

Karen Schweitzer has written numerous articles for magazines and newspapers, such as the *Erickson Tribune* and *Learning Through History*, and for Web sites like About.com. She is also the author of several books, including *The Shih Tzu* and *Shaun White*. Karen lives in Michigan with her husband. You can learn more about her at www.karenschweitzer.com.

PICTURE CREDITS